# ELON MUSK THE REVOLUTIONARY MAN

**"AT THE END OF THE DAY, WHETHER OR NOT THOSE PEOPLE ARE COMFORTABLE WITH HOW YOU'RE LIVING YOUR LIFE DOESN'T MATTER. WHAT MATTERS IS WHETHER YOU'RE COMFORTABLE WITH IT."**

**ADARSH KUMAR**

# Contents

# Preface

How thw world is growing rapidely it seems to be futuristic . watching all this i decided to write book on Elon musk for the new generation to know that how struggle musk has done fot it. it was hard to find article on him but i took support of internet and i got it . it took 24 days to complete book . and this my best book i have ever published so, it must be chnaged and it is very short and brief about Elon musk .

# Prologue

*The character on which the book is written don't need ant introduction he is modt richest person in the world and run several companies at a time and have net worth of 22,770 crores USD. a south african man who has no collage degree have came across by his talent thats why i am forced to write book on him .*

Enter Caption

CHAPTER ONE

# BRIEF ABOUT ELON MUSK

Elon Reeve Musk FRS ( born June 28, 1971) is a business magnate and investor. He is the founder, CEO, and Chief Engineer at SpaceX; angel investor, CEO, and Product Architect of Tesla, Inc.; founder of The Boring Company; and co-founder of Neuralink and OpenAI. With an estimated net worth of around US$203 billion as of June 2022, Musk is the wealthiest person in the world according to both the Bloomberg Billionaires Index and the Forbes real-time billionaires list.

Musk was born to White South African parents in Pretoria, where he grew up. He briefly attended the University of Pretoria before moving to Canada at age 17, acquiring citizenship through his Canadian-born mother. He matriculated at Queen's University and transferred to the University of Pennsylvania two years later, where he received bachelor's degrees in Economics and Physics. He moved to California in 1995 to attend Stanford University but decided instead to pursue a business career, co-founding the web software company Zip2 with his brother Kimbal. The startup was acquired by Compaq for $307 million in 1999. The same year, Musk co-founded online bank X.com, which merged with Confinity in 2000 to form PayPal. The company was bought by eBay in 2002 for $1.5 billion.

In 2002, Musk founded SpaceX, an aerospace manufacturer and space transport services company, of which he serves as CEO and Chief Engineer. In 2004, he was an early investor in electric vehicle manufacturer Tesla Motors, Inc. (now Tesla, Inc.). He became its chairman and product architect, eventually assuming the position of CEO in 2008. In 2006, he helped create SolarCity, a solar energy company that was later acquired by Tesla and became Tesla Energy. In 2015, he co-founded OpenAI, a nonprofit research company that promotes friendly artificial intelligence (AI). In 2016, he co-founded Neuralink, a neurotechnology company focused on developing brain–computer interfaces, and founded The Boring Company, a tunnel construction company. He also agreed to purchase the major American social networking service Twitter in 2022 for $44 billion. Musk has proposed the Hyperloop, a high-speed vactrain transportation system. He is the president of the Musk Foundation, an organization which donates to scientific research and education.

Musk has been criticized for making unscientific and controversial statements, such as spreading misinformation about the COVID-19 pandemic. In 2018, he was sued by the US Securities and Exchange Commission (SEC) for falsely tweeting that he had secured funding for a private takeover of Tesla; he settled with the SEC but did not admit guilt, and he temporarily stepped down from his Tesla chairmanship. In 2019, he won a defamation case brought against him by a British caver who had advised in the Tham Luang cave rescue

CHAPTER TWO

# CHILDHOOD AND FAMILY

Elon Reeve Musk was born on June 28, 1971, in Pretoria, a segregated suburb of apartheid South Africa. His mother is Maye Musk (née Haldeman), a model and dietitian born in Saskatchewan, Canada, but raised in South Africa. His father is Errol Musk, a White South African electromechanical engineer, pilot, sailor, consultant, and property developer who was once a half-owner of a Zambian emerald mine near Lake Tanganyika. Musk has a younger brother, Kimbal (born 1972), and a younger sister, Tosca (born 1974). His maternal grandfather, Joshua Haldeman, was an adventurous American-born Canadian who took his family on record-breaking journeys in a single-engine Bellanca airplane to Africa and Australia. Musk has British and Pennsylvania Dutch ancestry.

As a child, Musk's adenoids were removed because doctors suspected that he was deaf, but his mother later decided that he was just thinking "in another world."The family was very wealthy in Elon's youth; Elon's father was also elected to the Pretoria City Council as a representative of the anti-apartheid Progressive Party, with the Musk children reportedly sharing their father's dislike of apartheid. In an interview with The New York Times, Errol said his children had good relationships with Black people, including their domestic staff. Musk decided not to participate in South Africa's mandatory military service because of the government's apartheid system. Musk said this contributed to his decision to leave South Africa shortly after graduating from high school.

After his parents divorced in 1980, Musk mostly lived with his father in Pretoria and elsewhere, a choice he made two years after the divorce and subsequently regretted. Musk has become estranged from his father.

He has a half-sister and a half-brother on his father's side.Elon attended an Anglican Sunday school in his youth.

Around age 10, Musk developed an interest in computing and video games and acquired a Commodore VIC-20.He learned computer programming using a manual and, at age 12, sold the code of a BASIC-based video game he created called Blastar to PC and Office Technology magazine for approximately $500. An awkward and introverted child, Musk was bullied throughout his childhood and was once hospitalized after a group of boys threw him down a flight of stairs[why?].He attended Waterkloof House Preparatory School and Bryanston High School before graduating from Pretoria Boys High School.

CHAPTER THREE

# EDUCATION

Aware that it would be easier to enter the United States from Canada, Musk applied for a Canadian passport by jus sanguinis, through his Canadian-born mother. While awaiting the documentation, he attended the University of Pretoria for five months; this allowed him to avoid mandatory service in the South African military.Musk arrived in Canada in June 1989, and lived with a second cousin in Saskatchewan for a year, working odd jobs at a farm near Waldeck and lumber-mill.In 1990, he entered Queen's University in Kingston, Ontario.Two years later, he transferred to the University of Pennsylvania, where he graduated in 1997 with a Bachelor of Arts degree in physics and a Bachelor of Science degree in economics from the Wharton School.

In 1994, Musk held two internships in Silicon Valley during the summer: at energy storage startup Pinnacle Research Institute, which researched electrolytic ultracapacitors for energy storage, and at the Palo Alto-based startup Rocket Science Games. In 1995, he was accepted to a Doctor of Philosophy (Ph.D.) program in materials science at Stanford University in California. Musk tried to get a job at Netscape but never received a response to his inquiries. He dropped out of Stanford after two days, deciding instead to join the Internet boom and launch an Internet startup.

CHAPTER FOUR

# BUSINESS CAREER

## Zip2

In 1995, Musk, his brother Kimbal, and Greg Kouri founded web software company Zip2 with funds borrowed from Musk's father.They housed the venture at a small rented office in Palo Alto.The company developed and marketed an Internet city guide for the newspaper publishing industry, with maps, directions, and yellow pages. Musk says that before the company became successful, he could not afford an apartment and instead rented an office and slept on the couch and showered at the YMCA, and shared one computer with his brother.

According to Musk, "The website was up during the day and I was coding it at night, seven days a week, all the time." The Musk brothers obtained contracts with The New York Times and the Chicago Tribune,and persuaded the board of directors to abandon plans for a merger with CitySearch. Musk's attempts to become CEO, a position held by its Chairman Rich Sorkin, were thwarted by the board. Compaq acquired Zip2 for $307 million in cash in February 1999, and Musk received $22 million for his 7-percent share.

## x.com and paypal

In 1999, Musk co-founded X.com, an online financial services and e-mail payment company. The startup was one of the first federally insured online banks, and, in its initial months of operation, over 200,000 customers joined the service. The company's investors regarded Musk as inexperienced and replaced him with Intuit CEO Bill Harris by the end of the year.The following year, X.com merged with online bank Confinity to avoid competition. Founded by Max Levchin and Peter Thiel, Confinity had its own money-transfer service, PayPal, which was more popular than X.com's service.

Within the merged company, Musk returned as CEO. Musk's preference for Microsoft software over Unix created a rift in the company and caused Thiel to resign. Due to resulting technological issues and lack of a cohesive business model, the board ousted Musk and replaced him with Thiel in September 2000. Under Thiel, the company focused on the PayPal service and was renamed PayPal in 2001.In 2002, PayPal was acquired by eBay for $1.5 billion in stock, of which Musk—the largest shareholder with 11.72% of shares—received $175.8 million. In 2017, Musk purchased the domain X.com from PayPal for an undisclosed amount, explaining it has sentimental value.

## spacex

In 2001, Musk became involved with the nonprofit Mars Society. He was inspired by plans to place a growth-chamber for plants on Mars and discussed funding the project himself. In October 2001, Musk traveled to Moscow with Jim Cantrell and Mike Griffin to buy refurbished intercontinental ballistic missiles (ICBMs) that could send the greenhouse payloads into space. He met with companies NPO Lavochkin and Kosmotras; however, Musk was seen as a novice and was even spat on by one of the Russian chief designers.

The group returned to the United States empty-handed. In February 2002, the group returned to Russia to look for three ICBMs. They had another meeting with Kosmotras and were offered one rocket for $8 million, which Musk rejected. Musk instead decided to start a company that could build affordable rockets. With $100 million of his early fortune, Musk founded Space Exploration Technologies Corp., traded as SpaceX, in May 2002.As of 2021, he remains the company's CEO and also holds the title of Chief Engineer.

SpaceX attempted its first launch of the Falcon 1 rocket in 2006, and although the rocket failed to reach Earth orbit, it was awarded a Commercial Orbital Transportation Services program contract from NASA later that year. After two more failed attempts, which reportedly caused Musk so much stress that he was "waking from nightmares, screaming and in physical pain", SpaceX succeeded in launching the Falcon 1 into orbit in 2008, making it the first private liquid-fuel rocket to do so. Later that year, SpaceX received a $1.6 billion Commercial Resupply Services program contract from NASA for 12 flights of its Falcon 9 rocket and Dragon spacecraft to the International Space Station, replacing the Space Shuttle after its 2011 retirement. In 2012 the Dragon vehicle berthed with the ISS, a first for a private enterprise.

Musk explains the planned capabilities of SpaceX Starship to NORAD and Air Force Space Command, 2019

Working towards its goal of reusable rockets, in 2015 SpaceX successfully landed the first stage of a Falcon 9. Landings were later achieved on an autonomous spaceport drone ship, an ocean-based recovery platform. In 2018 SpaceX launched the Falcon Heavy; the inaugural mission carried Musk's personal Tesla Roadster as a dummy payload. In 2017 SpaceX unveiled its next-generation launch vehicle and spacecraft system, Big Falcon Rocket, later renamed to Starship, which would support all SpaceX launch service provider capabilities. In 2018 SpaceX announced a planned 2023 lunar circumnavigation mission, a private flight called dearMoon project. In 2020 SpaceX launched its first crewed flight, the Demo-2, becoming the first private company to place a person into orbit and dock a crewed spacecraft with the ISS.

SpaceX began development of the Starlink constellation of low Earth orbit satellites in 2015 to provide satellite Internet access, with the first two prototype satellites launched in February 2018. A second set of test satellites and the first large deployment of a piece of the constellation occurred in May 2019, when the first 60 operational satellites were launched. The total cost of the decade-long project to design, build, and deploy the constellation is estimated by SpaceX to be about $10 billion. During the 2022 Russian invasion of Ukraine, Musk sent Starlink systems to Ukraine to provide internet access and communication,an action praised by Ukrainian president Volodymyr Zelenskyy. However, he refused to block Russian state media on Starlink, declaring himself "a free speech absolutist."

The company has attracted criticism from astronomers who say Starlink's satellites are blocking the view of the skies, and from experts arguing that they risk colliding and causing dangers in space. In 2021, the International Astronomical Union petitioned the United Nations to protect the night sky from satellite constellations (including Starlink), and later created its own center to protect "the dark and quiet sky from satellite constellations".

## Musk said money and intelligence don't lead to success - these 3 things do

You need more than intelligence and money to be highly successful. In fact, these two components make up just a small fraction of success, according to entrepreneur Jim Cantrell, who was part of billionaire Elon Musk's SpaceX founding team.

In a Quora post that was first published on Forbes, Cantrell writes, "Intelligence is more of a tool that enables you to be successful rather than an ingredient itself."

Today, SpaceX is set to launch a rocket that, if successful, will carry Musk's cherry red Tesla Roadster to space.

"If we are successful in this, it is game over for all the other heavy lift rockets," Musk said Monday evening on a press call, reports Business Insider.

Through Cantrell's years of experience advising billionaires and tech companies, and his extensive work with Musk, he has seen what works and what doesn't work on the road to success.

Success, Cantrell writes, relies on a "single simple formula" that is based on three things, which Bill Gates, Mark Cuban and Jeff Bezos seem to agree on as well:

### *Passion*

Cantrell says to do what you're most passionate about in life. "Without passion, your work is not your love and you can never be your best or be better than others who are running with their passion," he writes.

Other highly successful people have said the same. In a Q&A with ABC.net, Microsoft co-founder Bill Gates says: "If you're lucky when you're very young, you find something you're passionate about. I did when I was 13 years old. I found computers and software."

This passion led him to create Microsoft, which is now valued at $507.5 billion and has made him the second richest person in the world with a net worth of $90.2 billion, according to Forbes.

## *Talent*

"Do something that you are inherently good at or talented at," writes Cantrell. If you spend your life doing something difficult, which you're not particularly good at, it will put you at a disadvantage to more talented people within that same field, he explains.

Billionaire entrepreneur Mark Cuban has said something similar. In fact, he says, talent and effort are often what lead to passion. For Cuban, technology was his talent. When he received his first job out of college, he started to use technology and realized he had a real knack for it, he wrote on his blog in 2012.

He taught himself how to use the software program at his company and would go up to eight hours without taking a break because he was so invested in his work.

"That's when I realized that I can be really, really good at technology," notes the "Shark Tank" star.

He eventually launched the computer consulting service, MicroSolutions, which he sold to CompuServe in 1990 for $6 million.

"When you are good at something, passionate and work even harder to excel and be the best at it, good things happen," writes Cuban, who now has a net worth of $3.3 billion, according to Forbes.

## *Value*

You could have the best idea in the world and be extremely enthusiastic about it, but if nobody wants it, then it's a dud, says Cantrell.

"Do something that creates value and can be sold into a market present or future," suggests the entrepreneur. Although creating a product or service can be "self satisfying," he writes, if nobody wants it, it won't "make you your fortune nor lead you to personal or professional success."

Amazon founder, and now the richest person in the world, Jeff Bezos prescribes to this theory. The retail giant was able to expand so quickly because Bezos offered a service that customers found valuable: a wide array of products on a convenient online platform.

When Amazon was first launched, it only sold books. Shortly after, the company added music and videos. Then Bezos reached out to customers to figure out what they really wanted to buy.

"The list came back incredibly long," Bezos tells Charlie Rose in a 2016 interview. But he listened to his consumers, giving them what they valued and were willing to pay for. This customer-obsession is now at the heart of the company's motto.

You could have the best idea in the world and be extremely enthusiastic about it, but if nobody wants it, then it's a dud, says Cantrell.

"Do something that creates value and can be sold into a market present or future," suggests the entrepreneur. Although creating a product or service can be "self satisfying," he writes, if nobody wants it, it won't "make you your fortune nor lead you to personal or professional success."

Amazon founder, and now the richest person in the world, Jeff Bezos prescribes to this theory. The retail giant was able to expand so quickly because Bezos offered a service that customers found valuable: a wide array of products on a convenient online platform.

When Amazon was first launched, it only sold books. Shortly after, the company added music and videos. Then Bezos reached out to customers to figure out what they really wanted to buy.

"The list came back incredibly long," Bezos tells Charlie Rose in a 2016 interview. But he listened to his consumers, giving them what they valued and were willing to pay for. This customer-obsession is now at the heart of the company's motto.

Here's the future Jeff Bezos saw for himself at 80, if he didn't found Amazon at 30

"We are always focused on the customer, working backwards from the customer's needs, developing new skills internally so that we can satisfy what we perceive to be future customer needs," Bezos tells Rose.

And it's clearly worked. Amazon is on track to become a $3 trillion company in a decade.

Cantrell emphasizes that in the list above, money and intelligence are not key factors. "If you combine these three elements into your pursuits in life," he writes, "you will be very successful and the money will come on its own."

Enter Caption

## Tesla

Tesla, Inc.—originally Tesla Motors—was incorporated in 2003 by Martin Eberhard and Marc Tarpenning, who financed the company until the Series A round of funding.Both men played active roles in the company's early development prior to Musk's involvement. Musk led the Series A round of investment in February 2004; he invested $6.5 million, became the majority shareholder, and joined Tesla's board of directors as chairman.Musk took an active role within the company and oversaw Roadster product design but was not deeply involved in day-to-day business operations.

Following a series of escalating conflicts in 2007 and the 2008 financial crisis, Eberhard was ousted from the firm.Musk assumed leadership of the company as CEO and product architect in 2008. A 2009 lawsuit settlement with Eberhard designated Musk as a Tesla co-founder, along with Tarpenning and two others. As of 2019, Musk was the longest tenured CEO of any automotive manufacturer globally. In 2021 Musk nominally changed his title to "Technoking" while retaining his position as CEO.

Tesla first built an electric sports car, the Roadster, in 2008. With sales of about 2,500 vehicles, it was the first serial production all-electric car to use lithium-ion battery cells. Tesla began delivery of its four-door Model S sedan in 2012; a cross-over, the Model X was launched in 2015. A mass market sedan, the Model 3, was released in 2017.The Model 3 is the all-time best-selling plug-in electric car worldwide, and, in June 2021, became the first electric car to sell 1 million units globally.A fifth vehicle, the Model Y crossover, was launched in 2020. The Cybertruck—an all-electric pickup truck—was unveiled in 2019. Under Musk, Tesla has also constructed multiple lithium-ion battery and electric vehicle factories, such as Gigafactory 1 in Nevada, Gigafactory 2 in New York, Gigafactory 3 in China, Gigafactory 4 in Germany and Gigafactory 5 in Texas.

Musk at the 2019 Tesla annual shareholder meeting

Since its initial public offering in 2010, Tesla stock has risen significantly; it became the most valuable carmaker in summer 2020, and it entered the S&P 500 later that year. In October 2021 it reached a market capitalization of $1 trillion, the sixth company to do so in US history. On November 6, 2021, Musk proposed on Twitter selling 10% of his Tesla stock, since "much is made lately of unrealized gains being a means of tax avoidance".After more than 3.5 million Twitter accounts supported the sale, Musk sold $6.9 billion of Tesla stock in the week ending November 12, and a total of $16.4 billion by year end, reaching the 10% target. In February 2022, The Wall Street Journal reported that both Elon and Kimbal Musk were under investigation by the SEC for possible insider trading related to the sale.

As the co-founder and CEO of Tesla, Elon leads all product design, engineering and global manufacturing of the company's electric vehicles, battery products and solar energy products.

Since the company's inception in 2003, Tesla's mission has been to accelerate the world's transition to sustainable energy. The first Tesla product, the Roadster sports car, debuted in 2008, followed by the Model S sedan, which was introduced in 2012, and the Model X SUV, which launched in 2015. Model S received Consumer Reports' Best Overall Car and has been named the Ultimate Car of the Year by Motor Trend, while Model X was the first SUV ever to earn 5-star safety ratings in every category and sub-category in the National Highway Traffic Safety Administration's tests. In 2017, Tesla began deliveries of Model 3, a mass-market electric vehicle with more than 320 miles of range, and unveiled Tesla Semi, which is designed to save owners at least $200,000 over a million miles based on fuel costs alone. In 2019, Tesla unveiled Cybertruck, which will have better utility than a traditional truck and more performance than a sports car, as well as the Model Y compact SUV, which began customer deliveries in early 2020.

Tesla also produces three energy storage products, the Powerwall home battery, the Powerpack commercial-scale battery, and Megapack, which is designed for utility-scale installations. In 2016, Tesla became the world's first vertically-integrated sustainable energy company with the acquisition of SolarCity, the leading provider of solar power systems in the United States, and in 2017 released Solar Roof – a beautiful and affordable energy generation product.

As lead designer at SpaceX, Elon oversees the development of rockets and spacecraft for missions to Earth orbit and ultimately to other planets. In 2008, the SpaceX Falcon 1 was the first privately developed liquid fuel rocket to reach orbit, and SpaceX made further history in 2017 by re-flying both a Falcon 9 rocket and Dragon spacecraft for the first time. Soon after, Falcon Heavy, the most powerful operational rocket in the world by a factor of two, completed its first flight in 2018. In 2019, SpaceX's crew-capable version of the Dragon spacecraft completed its first demonstration mission, and the company will fly NASA astronauts to the International Space Station for the first time in 2020. Building on these achievements, SpaceX is developing Starship – a fully reusable transportation system that will carry crew and cargo to the Moon, Mars and beyond – and Starlink, which will deliver high speed broadband internet to locations where access has been unreliable, expensive, or completely unavailable. By pioneering reusable rockets, SpaceX is pursuing the long-term goal of making humans a multi-planet species by creating a self-sustaining city on Mars.

Elon is also CEO of Neuralink, which is developing ultra-high bandwidth brain-machine interfaces to connect the human brain to computers.

He also launched The Boring Company, which combines fast, affordable tunneling technology with an all-electric public transportation system in order to alleviate soul-crushing urban congestion and enable high-speed, long-distance travel. The Boring Company built a 1.15 mile R&D tunnel in Hawthorne, and is currently constructing Vegas Loop, a public transportation system at the Las Vegas Convention Center.

## Sec lawsuit

In September 2018, Musk was sued by the SEC for a tweet claiming funding had been secured for potentially taking Tesla private. The lawsuit characterized the tweet as false, misleading, and damaging to investors, and sought to bar Musk from serving as CEO of publicly traded companies. Two days later, Musk settled with the SEC, without admitting or denying the SEC's allegations. As a result, Musk and Tesla were fined $20 million each, and Musk was forced to step down for three years as Tesla chairman but was able to remain as CEO.

Musk has stated in interviews he does not regret posting the tweet that triggered the SEC investigation. On February 19, 2019, Musk stated in a tweet that Tesla would build half a million cars in 2019.The SEC reacted to Musk's tweet by filing in court, initially asking the court to hold him in contempt for violating the terms of a settlement agreement with such a tweet, which was disputed by Musk. This was eventually settled by a joint agreement between Musk and the SEC clarifying the previous agreement details. The agreement included a list of topics that Musk would need preclearance before tweeting about. In May 2020, a judge prevented a lawsuit from proceeding that claimed a tweet by Musk regarding Tesla stock price ("too high imo") violated the agreement. FOIA released records showing that the SEC itself concluded Musk has subsequently violated the agreement twice by tweeting regarding "Tesla's solar roof production volumes and its stock price".

## *Solarcity and tesla energy*

Musk provided the initial concept and financial capital for SolarCity, which his cousins Lyndon and Peter Rive co-founded in 2006. By 2013, SolarCity was the second largest provider of solar power systems in the United States. In 2014 Musk promoted the idea of SolarCity building an advanced production facility in Buffalo, New York, triple the size of the largest solar plant in the United States.Construction on the factory started in 2014 and was completed in 2017. It operated as a joint venture with Panasonic until early 2020 when Panasonic departed.

Tesla acquired SolarCity for over $2 billion in 2016 and merged it with its battery unit to create Tesla Energy. The announcement of the deal resulted in a more than 10% drop in Tesla's stock price. At the time, SolarCity was facing liquidity issues.Multiple shareholder groups filed a lawsuit against Musk and Tesla's directors, claiming that the purchase of

SolarCity was done solely to benefit Musk and came at the expense of Tesla and its shareholders. Tesla directors settled the lawsuit in January 2020, leaving Musk the sole remaining defendant.Two years later, the court ruled in musk favour.

## *Neuralink*

In 2016, Musk co-founded Neuralink, a neurotechnology startup company to integrate the human brain with artificial intelligence (AI) by creating devices that are embedded in the human brain to facilitate its merging with machines. The devices will also reconcile with the latest improvements in AI to stay updated. Such improvements could enhance memory or allow the devices to communicate with software more effectively.

At a 2020 live demonstration, Musk described one of their early devices as "a Fitbit in your skull" that could soon cure paralysis, deafness, blindness, and other disabilities. Many neuroscientists and publications criticized these claims;MIT Technology Review described them as "highly speculative" and "neuroscience theater".

## *The boring company*

In 2017, Musk founded The Boring Company to construct tunnels. Early that year, the company began discussions with regulatory bodies and initiated construction of a 30-foot (9.1 m) wide, 50-foot (15 m) long, and 15-foot (4.6 m) deep "test trench" on the premises of SpaceX's offices as it required no permits. A tunnel beneath the Las Vegas Convention Center was completed in early 2021.Local officials have approved further expansions of the tunnel system.

As a merchandising and publicity stunt, The Boring Company sold 2,000 novelty flamethrowers in 2018. The idea was inspired by the Mel Brooks-directed film Spaceballs (1987).

## *Twitter*

Since joining the social media platform in 2009, Musk has been an active user of Twitter, where he has over 95 million followers. He posts memes, promotes his business interests, and comments on contemporary political and cultural issues.

As early as 2017, Musk tweeted interest in buying the platform. In January 2022, Musk began buying significant quantities of shares in the company, reaching a 5% stake in the company in March. Musk reached a total of 73,115,038 shares on April 1, 9.13% of Twitter's overall shares, valued at the time at $2.64 billion, making him the largest shareholder in the company. It is alleged that Musk did not file the necessary paperwork to notify the SEC within 10 days of when his stake in the company surpassed 5%, a violation of US securities laws.On May 27, 2022, the SEC published the letter that was sent to Musk on April 4, where his acquisition of a 9.2% stake in Twitter was questioned, confirming that Musk was late in filing the paperwork. When Musk publicly disclosed his investment in a Securities and Exchange Commission 13G filing on April 4, 2022, Twitter shares experienced the largest intraday surge since its 2013 IPO. The revelation that Musk had acquired a significant stake in Twitter followed Musk's March tweets in which he questioned Twitter's commitment to freedom of speech and said he was considering developing a rival social media site, although the comments were made after he had acquired 7.5% of the company.

On April 4, Musk agreed to a deal that would see him appointed to Twitter's board of directors and prohibit him from acquiring more than 14.9% of the company. However, on April 13, Musk made a $43 billion offer to buy Twitter, launching a takeover bid to buy 100% of Twitter's stock at $54.20 per share. In a letter to Twitter's board, he argued that a private Twitter would thrive and best advance free speech.In response, Twitter's board adopted a shareholder rights plan to make it significantly more expensive for any single investor to own more than 15% of the company without approval of the board. A week later, Musk secured funding worth $46.5 billion,which included $12.5 billion in loans against his stock in Tesla and $21 billion in equity financing.Later that same day, Musk successfully concluded his bid to buy Twitter and bring the company private for approximately $44 billion.

Tesla's stock market value sank by more than $125 billion the next day in reaction to the deal, causing Musk to lose around $30 billion of his net worth. He subsequently tweeted criticism of Twitter executive Vijaya Gadde's policies to his 86 million followers, which led to some of them engaging in sexist and racist harassment against her. Exactly a month after announcing the takeover, Musk stated that the deal was "on hold" following a report that 5 percent of Twitter's daily active users were spam accounts, causing Twitter shares to drop more than 10 percent.He later clarified that he remained committed to the acquisition.

## *managerial style and treatment of employees*

Musk's managerial style and treatment of employees have been heavily criticized.The Wall Street Journal reported that, after Musk insisted on branding his vehicles as "self-driving", he faced criticism from his engineers, some of whom resigned in response, with one stating that Musk's "reckless decision making... ha potentially put customer lives at risk". The New York Times characterized Musk's managerial style as impetuous, operating on impulse and "the belief that he is absolutely right". The 2021 book Power Play contains multiple anecdotes of Musk berating employees.Wired News reported that Tesla employees were told not to walk past Musk's desk because of his "wild firing rampages"

CHAPTER FIVE

# OTHER ACTIVITIES

## *Hyperloop*

In 2013, Musk announced plans for a version of a vactrain (or vacuum tube train), assigning a dozen engineers from Tesla and SpaceX to establish the conceptual foundations and create initial designs. On August 12, 2013, Musk unveiled the concept, which he dubbed the hyperloop. The alpha design for the system was published in a whitepaper posted to the Tesla and SpaceX blogs. The document scoped out the technology and outlined a notional route where such a transport system could be built between the Greater Los Angeles Area and the San Francisco Bay Area at an estimated cost of $6 billion.The proposal, if technologically feasible at the costs he has cited, would make Hyperloop travel cheaper than any other mode of transport for such long distances.

In June 2015, Musk announced a design competition for students and others to build Hyperloop pods to operate on a SpaceX-sponsored mile-long track in a 2015–2017 Hyperloop pod competition. The track was used in January 2017, and Musk also announced that the company started a tunnel project with Hawthorne airport as its destination. In July 2017, Musk claimed that he had received "verbal government approval" to build a hyperloop from New York City to Washington, D.C., stopping in both Philadelphia and Baltimore. Mention of the project for the DC to Baltimore part were removed from the Boring Company website later in 2021.

## *Openal*

In 2015, Musk founded OpenAI, a not-for-profit AI research company aiming to develop artificial general intelligence intended to be safe and beneficial to humanity. A particular focus of the company is to "counteract large corporations [and governments] who may gain too much power by owning super-intelligence systems". In 2018, Musk left the OpenAI board to avoid possible future conflicts with his role as CEO of Tesla as the company increasingly became involved in AI through Tesla Autopilot.

## *Tham launge cave rescue & defamation case*

In July 2018, Musk arranged for his employees to build a mini-submarine to assist the rescue of children stuck in a flooded cavern in Thailand. Richard Stanton, leader of the international rescue diving team, urged Musk to facilitate the construction of the vehicle as a back-up, in case flooding worsened.

Engineers at SpaceX and The Boring Company built the mini-submarine out of a Falcon 9 liquid oxygen transfer tube in eight hours and personally delivered it to Thailand. By this time, however, eight of the 12 children had already been rescued using full face masks and oxygen under anesthesia; consequently Thai authorities declined to use the submarine. Musk was later one of the 187 people who received various honors conferred by the King of Thailand in March 2019 for involvement in the rescue effort, e.g. the Order of the Direkgunabhorn.

Soon after the rescue, Vernon Unsworth, a British recreational caver who had been exploring the cave for the previous six years and played a key advisory role in the operation, criticized the submarine on CNN as amounting to nothing more than a public relations effort with no chance of success, and that Musk "had no conception of what the cave passage was like" and "can stick his submarine where it hurts". Musk asserted on Twitter that the device would have worked and referred to Unsworth as a "pedo guy" .He deleted the tweets, and apologized, along with responses to critical tweets from Cher Scarlett, a software engineer, which had caused his followers to harass her. In an email to BuzzFeed News Musk later called Unsworth a "child rapist" and said that he had married a child.

In September, Unsworth filed a defamation suit in Los Angeles federal court. In his defense, Musk argued that "'pedo guy' was a common insult used in South Africa when I was growing up ... synonymous with 'creepy old man' and is used to insult a person's appearance and demeanor". The defamation case began in December 2019, with Unsworth seeking $190 million in damages. During the trial Musk apologized to Unsworth again for the tweet. On December 6, the jury found in favor of Musk and ruled he was not liable.

## *2018 Joe Rogan podcast appearance*

In September 2018, Musk appeared on The Joe Rogan Experience podcast and discussed various topics for over two hours. During the interview, Musk sampled a puff from a cigar consisting, Joe Rogan claimed, of tobacco laced with cannabis. Tesla stock dropped after the incident, which coincided with the confirmation of the departure of Tesla's vice president of worldwide finance earlier that day.Fortune wondered if the cannabis use could have ramifications for SpaceX contracts with the United States Air Force, though an Air Force spokesperson told The Verge that there was no investigation and that the Air Force was still processing the situation. In a 60 Minutes interview, Musk said of the incident: "I do not smoke pot. As anybody who watched that podcast could tell, I have no idea how to smoke pot."

## *Music ventures*

In 2019, Musk released a rap track, "RIP Harambe", on SoundCloud as Emo G Records. The track, which is an allusion to the killing of Harambe, a gorilla in a Cincinnati zoo, and the subsequent "tasteless" Internet sensationalism surrounding the event, was performed by Yung Jake, written by Yung Jake and Caroline Polachek, and produced by BloodPop. The following year, Musk released an EDM track, "Don't Doubt Ur Vibe", featuring his own lyrics and vocals. While The Guardian critic Alexi Petridis described it as "indistinguishable... from umpteen competent but unthrilling bits of bedroom electronica posted elsewhere on Soundcloud", TechCrunch said it was "not a bad representation of the genre".

## *Philanthropy*

In 2012, Musk took the Giving Pledge, thereby committing to give the majority of his wealth to charitable causes either during his lifetimes or in his will. He has endowed prizes at the X Prize Foundation, including $15 million to encourage innovation in addressing illiteracy and $100 million to reward improved carbon capture technology.

In 2020, Forbes gave Musk a philanthropy score of 1, because he had given away less than 1% of his net worth. In November 2021, Musk donated $5.7 billion of Tesla's shares to charity; however, Fortune magazine noted that no nonprofits subsequently announced receiving any money from Musk, despite his November 2021 regulatory filing citing earmarking 5.7 billion worth of his Tesla shares for charity.

## *Musk Foundation*

Musk is president of the Musk Foundation, which states its purpose is to provide solar-power energy systems in disaster areas; support research, development, and advocacy (for interests including human space exploration, pediatrics, renewable energy and "safe artificial intelligence"); and support science and engineering educational efforts. Since 2002, the foundation has made over 350 contributions. Around half were to scientific research or education nonprofits. Notable beneficiaries include the Wikimedia Foundation, his alma mater the University of Pennsylvania, and Kimbal's Big Green. Vox described the foundation as "almost entertaining in its simplicity and yet is strikingly opaque", noting that its website was only 33 words in plain-text. The foundation has been criticized for the relatively small amount of wealth donated. From 2002 to 2018, it gave out $25 million directly to non-profits, nearly half of which went to Musk's OpenAI, which was at the time a non-profit organization.

The Musk Foundation is a private grantmaking foundation founded in 2002 by technology entrepreneur Elon Musk and his brother, Kimbal. The brothers are the foundation's sole officers; Elon Musk is president and board director and Kimbal Musk is secretary, treasurer, and board director.

According to its website, the Musk Foundation makes grants in support of five areas, some of which intersect with Musk's business ventures: “renewable energy research and advocacy,” “human space exploration research and advocacy,” “pediatric research,” “science and engineering education,” and “development of safe artificial intelligence to benefit humanity. Charitable recipients of Musk Foundation grants include international aid nonprofits such as Doctors Without Borders, healthcare organizations such as World Spine Care, and the co-educational Mirman School for Gifted Children.

CHAPTER SIX

# WEALTH

Musk made $175.8 million when PayPal was sold to eBay in 2002. He was first listed on the Forbes Billionaires List in 2012, with a net worth of $2 billion.

At the start of 2020, Musk had a net worth of $27 billion. By the year's end his net worth had increased by $150 billion, largely driven by his ownership of around 20% of Tesla stock. During this, Musk's net worth was often volatile. For example, it dropped $16.3 billion in September, the largest single-day plunge in the history of the Bloomberg Billionaires Index. In November of that year, Musk passed Facebook co-founder Mark Zuckerberg to become the third-richest person in the world; a week later he passed Microsoft co-founder Bill Gates to become the second-richest.In January 2021, Musk, with a net worth of $185 billion, surpassed Amazon founder Jeff Bezos to become the richest person in the world. Bezos reclaimed the top spot the following month. On September 27, 2021, Forbes announced that Musk had a net worth of over $200 billion, and was the richest person in the world, after Tesla stock surged. In November 2021, Musk became the first person with a net worth over $300 billion.

Around three-quarters of Musk's wealth derives from Tesla. Musk does not receive a salary from Tesla; he agreed in 2018 to a compensation plan with the board that ties his personal earnings to Tesla's valuation and revenue.The deal stipulated that Musk only receives the compensation if Tesla reaches certain market values.It was the largest such deal ever done between a CEO and board. In the first award, given in May 2020, he was eligible to purchase 1.69 million TSLA shares (about 1% of the company) at below-market prices, which was worth about $800 million.

Musk paid $455 million in taxes on $1.52 billion of income between 2014 and 2018. According to ProPublica, Musk paid no federal income taxes in 2018.He claimed his 2021 tax bill was estimated at $12 billion based on his sale of $14 billion worth of Tesla stock.

Musk has repeatedly described himself as "cash poor", and has "professed to have little interest in the material trappings of wealth". In 2012, Musk signed The Giving Pledge and, in May 2020, pledged to "sell almost all physical possessions". In 2021 Musk defended his wealth by saying he is "accumulating resources to help make life multiplanetary [and] extend the light of consciousness to the stars". In 2003, Musk said his favorite plane he owned was the L-39 Albatros. He uses a private jet owned by SpaceX and acquired a second jet in August 2020. The jet's heavy use of fossil fuels—it flew over 150,000 miles in 2018—has received criticism despite its utility in quickly traveling between widely flung businesses.

CHAPTER SEVEN

# OPINIONS

## *Politics*

Although often described as libertarian, Musk has called himself "politically moderate" and was a registered independent when he lived in California. The New York Times noted that Musk "expresses views that don't fit neatly into [the American] binary, left-right political framework." Historically, Musk has donated to both Democrats and Republicans, many of whom are in states in which he has a vested interest. Musk has also been described as having a "charm offensive" to woo China and its markets for Tesla.

Musk voted for Hillary Clinton in the 2016 U.S. presidential election. In the 2020 Democratic presidential primaries, Musk endorsed candidate Andrew Yang and expressed support for his proposed universal basic income. He also endorsed Kanye West's independent campaign in the 2020 general election, but ultimately voted for Joe Biden in 2020. In 2022, Musk said that he could "no longer support" the Democrats, and leaned towards supporting Republican Ron DeSantis in the 2024 U.S. presidential election if he were a candidate.

Prompted by the emergence of artificial intelligence, Musk has voiced support for a universal basic income. He supported targeting an inclusive tax rate of 40%, preferred consumption taxes to income taxes, and supported the estate tax. Musk opposed a "billionaire tax",and has tweeted insults at more progressive Democratic politicians like Bernie Sanders,Alexandria Ocasio-Cortez, and Elizabeth Warren.

Musk's statements often provoked controversy, such as for mocking preferred gender pronouns,[comparing Canadian prime minister Justin Trudeau to Adolf Hitler in support of the 2022 Canada convoy protest,and saying that the U.S. can "coup whoever we want".

## *Sustainability of life on Earth & Mars colonization*

Musk and Mohammad Al Gergawi at the 2017 World Government Summit

Musk has described climate change as the greatest threat to humanity after AI,and has advocated for a carbon tax.Musk criticized then-president Donald Trump for his stance on climate change and after joining Trump's two business advisory councils, Musk resigned from both in 2017 in protest against Trump's decision to withdraw the United States from the Paris Agreement.

Musk has long promoted the colonization of Mars and argues that humanity should become a "multiplanetary species". He has envisaged the use of nuclear weapons to terraform Mars. He envisioned enacting a direct democracy on Mars with a system in which more votes would be required to create laws than remove them.

Musk has also voiced concerns about human population decline, saying that "Mars has zero human population. We need a lot of people to become a multiplanet civilization."Speaking at The Wall Street Journal's CEO Council session in December 2021, Musk stated that declining birth rates and population is one of the biggest risks to human civilization.

## *Technology*

Musk has frequently spoken about the hypothetical existential threat AI poses to humanity. Musk's opinions about AI have provoked controversy and have been criticized by experts such as Yann LeCun, who claimed Musk's panic was influenced by reading Nick Bostrom's book Superintelligence, and by Musk's attraction to the idea that he will save humanity.Facebook's head of AI Jerome Pesenti said that Musk "has no idea what he's talking about when he talks about AI." He noted that Musk's comments about a future machine takeover distracts people from real, immediate AI concerns, such as AI algorithms exacerbating inequality. Consequently, according to CNBC, Musk is "not always looked upon favorably" by the AI research community.Mark Zuckerberg has clashed with Musk on the issue and called his AI warnings "pretty irresponsible".

Musk has claimed that humans are probably living in a computer simulation. Musk has said he cannot see the appeal of a virtual reality-driven metaverse.

Despite The Boring Company's involvement in building mass transit infrastructure, Musk has criticized public transport and promoted individualized transport (private vehicles). His comments have been called "elitist" and have sparked widespread criticism from both transportation and urban planning experts, who have pointed out that public transportation in dense urban areas is more economical, more energy efficient, and requires much less space than private cars.

## *COVID-19*

Musk was criticized for his public comments and conduct related to the COVID-19 pandemic. He spread misinformation about the virus, including promoting a widely discredited paper on the benefits of chloroquine and a study that suggested doctors inflated COVID-19 case numbers for financial gain.

In March 2020, Musk stated, "The coronavirus panic is dumb." In an email to Tesla employees, Musk referred to COVID-19 as a "specific form of the common cold" and predicted that confirmed COVID-19 cases would not exceed 0.1% of the US population.On March 19, 2020, Musk predicted that there would be "probably close to zero new cases in [the US] by end of April".Politico labeled this statement one of "the most audacious, confident and spectacularly incorrect prognostications [of 2020]". Musk also claimed falsely that children "are essentially immune" to COVID-19.

Musk repeatedly condemned COVID-19 lockdowns and refused to close the Tesla Fremont factory in March 2020, defying the local shelter-in-place order. In May 2020, he reopened the Tesla factory, defying the local stay-at-home order, and warned workers that they would be unpaid and their pandemic unemployment benefits might be jeopardized if they did not report to work.

In March 2020, Musk promised that Tesla would make ventilators for COVID-19 patients if there was a shortage. After figures like New York City mayor Bill de Blasio responded to Musk's offer, Musk said he thought the ventilators which Tesla was working on would probably be unneeded.Later, Musk offered to donate ventilators which Tesla would build or buy from a third party. However, instead of the much more expensive and sought-after invasive mechanical ventilator (IMV) machines, Musk eventually bought and donated medical devices that hospitals noted were BiPAP and CPAP machines.

In September 2020, Musk stated that he would not get the COVID-19 vaccine, because he and his children were "not at risk for COVID". Two months later, Musk contracted COVID-19 and suggested his COVID-19 rapid antigen test results were dubious, after which the phrase "Space Karen" trended on Twitter, in reference to Musk.However, in December 2021, Musk revealed that he and his eligible children had received the vaccine.

## *Finance*

Musk has stated that he does not believe the US government should provide subsidies to companies; instead they should use a carbon tax to discourage poor behavior.Musk says that the free market would achieve the best solution, and that producing environmentally unfriendly vehicles should come with its own consequences. His stance has been called hypocritical as Tesla has received billions of dollars in subsidies. In addition, Tesla made large sums from government-initiated systems of zero emissions credits offered in California and the United States federal level, which enabled improved initial consumer adoption of Tesla vehicles, as the tax credits given by governments enabled Tesla's battery electric vehicles to be price-competitive, in relative comparison with existing lower-priced internal combustion engine vehicles.[391] Notably, Tesla generates a sizeable portion of its revenue from its sales of carbon credits granted to the company, by both the European Union Emissions Trading System and the Chinese national carbon trading scheme.

Musk, a longtime opponent of short-selling, has repeatedly criticized the practice and argued it should be illegal. Musk's opposition to short-selling has been speculated to stem from how short-sellers often organize and publish opposition research about the companies that they believe are currently overvalued. In early 2021, he encouraged the GameStop short squeeze.

## *Cryptocurrency*

Musk has promoted cryptocurrencies, stating that he supports them over traditional government-issued fiat currencies. Given the influence of Musk's tweets on moving cryptocurrency markets, his statements around cryptocurrencies have been viewed as market manipulations by some, such as the critic Nouriel Roubini. Musk's social media praising of Bitcoin and Dogecoin was credited for increasing their prices. Consequently, Tesla's 2021 announcement that it bought $1.5 billion worth of Bitcoin raised questions against the backdrop of Musk's social media behavior.Tesla's announcement that it would accept Bitcoin for payment was criticized by environmentalists and investors due to the environmental impact of cryptocurrency mining; in 2021, the energy consumption of Bitcoin mining, which has built-in energy inefficiency, exceeded that of Argentina. A few months later, in response to the criticism, Musk announced on Twitter that Tesla would no longer accept Bitcoin and would not engage in any Bitcoin transactions until the environmental issues are solved.

CHAPTER EIGHT

# PERSONAL LIFE

From the early 2000s until late 2020, Musk resided in California where both Tesla and SpaceX were founded and where their headquarters are still located.In 2020, he moved to Texas, stating that California had become "complacent" with its economic success.

While hosting Saturday Night Live in May 2021, Musk stated that he has Asperger syndrome. The BBC wrote, "It is thought to be the first time Mr Musk has spoken about his condition."

## *Marriages, dating life, and children*

Musk met his first wife, Canadian Justine Wilson, while attending Queen's University, and they married in 2000. He contracted malaria in 2000 while on vacation in South Africa, and nearly died. In 2002, their first child died of sudden infant death syndrome (SIDS) at the age of 10 weeks.After his death, the couple decided to use IVF to continue their family.They had twins in 2004 followed by triplets in 2006. The couple divorced in 2008 and shared custody of their children.One of their children filed a request in April 2022 for a name change to reflect her gender identity, and because she no longer wished to be associated with Musk, her biological father.

In 2008, Musk began dating English actor Talulah Riley. They married in September 2010 at Dornoch Cathedral in Scotland. In 2012, he announced a divorce from Riley. In 2013, Musk and Riley remarried. In December 2014, he filed for a second divorce from Riley; however, the action was withdrawn. A second divorce was finalized in 2016. Musk then dated Amber Heard for several months in 2017; he had reportedly been pursuing her since 2012. Musk was later accused by Johnny Depp of having an affair with Heard while she was still married to Depp. Musk and Heard both denied the affair.

In 2018, Musk and Canadian musician Grimes revealed that they were dating. Grimes gave birth to their son in May 2020. According to Musk and Grimes, his name was "X Æ A-12"; however, the name would have violated California regulations as it contained characters that are not in the modern English alphabet, and was then changed to "X Æ A-Xii". This drew more confusion, as Æ is not a letter in the modern English alphabet. The child was eventually named "X AE A-XII" Musk, with "X" as a first name, "AE A-XII" as a middle name, and "Musk" as surname. Musk confirmed reports that the couple are "semi-separated" in September 2021; in an interview with Time in December 2021, he said he was single. In March 2022, Grimes said of her relationship with Musk: "I would probably refer to him as my boyfriend, but we're very fluid." She further revealed that their first daughter was born in December 2021 via surrogate. Later that month, Grimes tweeted that she and Musk had broken up again "but he's my best friend and the love of my life."

## *Sexual misconduct allegation*

In May 2022, a Business Insider article alleged that Musk engaged in sexual misconduct with a SpaceX flight attendant in a private jet in 2016. According to the article, citing an anonymous friend of a flight attendant, in November 2018, Musk, SpaceX and the former flight attendant entered into a severance agreement granting the attendant a $250,000 payment in exchange for a promise not to sue over the claims.

Musk stated, "If I were inclined to engage in sexual harassment, this is unlikely to be the first time in my entire 30-year career that it comes to light". Musk accused the article from Business Insider of being a "politically motivated hit piece".He also suggested that the scandal should be known as "Elongate".[undue weight? – discuss]

After the release of the Business Insider article, Tesla's stock fell by more than 6%, decreasing Musk's net worth by $10 billion. The financial newspaper Barron's wrote "...some investors considered key-man risk - the danger that a company could be badly hurt by the loss of one individual."

## Public recognition

## *In popular culture*

Musk has made multiple cameos and appearances in films such as Iron Man 2 (2010), Machete Kills (2013), Why Him? (2016), and Men in Black: International (2019). Television series on which he has appeared include The Simpsons ("The Musk Who Fell to Earth", 2015),The Big Bang Theory ("The Platonic Permutation", 2015), South Park ("Members Only", 2016), Rick and Morty ("One Crew over the Crewcoo's Morty", 2019), Young Sheldon ("A Patch, a Modem, and a Zantac®", 2017) and Saturday Night Live (2021). He has contributed interviews to the documentaries Racing Extinction (2015) and the Werner Herzog-directed Lo and Behold (2016).

In China, Musk has become a "trademark phenomenon" according to SCMP, with over 270 different companies having registered trademarks using his English name or Chinese transliteration, for a multitude of products including printing, restaurants, textiles, and design.

## *Accolades*

Main article: List of awards and honors received by Elon Musk

Musk was elected a fellow of the Royal Society (FRS) in 2018. In 2015 he received an honorary doctorate in engineering and technology at Yale and IEEE Honorary Membership. Awards for his contributions to the development of the Falcon rockets include the American Institute of Aeronautics and Astronautics George Low Transportation Award in 2008, the Fédération Aéronautique Internationale Gold Space Medal in 2010, and the Royal Aeronautical Society Gold Medal in 2012. He was listed among Time magazine's 100 Most Influential People in 2010,2013, 2018, and 2021. Musk was selected as Time's "Person of the Year" for 2021. Time editor-in-chief Edward Felsenthal wrote that "Person of the Year is a marker of influence, and few individuals have had more influence than Musk on life on Earth, and potentially life off Earth too". In 2022, Musk was elected as a member into the National Academy of Engineering.

CHAPTER NINE

# ARTICLES ON MUSK

### *Elon Musk 'overcome with emotion' after SpaceX's 1st astronaut launch*

*By Hanneke Weitering*

SpaceX founder Elon Musk celebrates after the successful launch of the Crew Dragon Demo-2 mission at NASA's Kennedy Space Center in Florida, on May 30, 2020.

SpaceX founder Elon Musk(opens in new tab) was choked up with emotion after his company successfully launched astronauts to space for the first time on Saturday (May 30).

"I'm really quite overcome with emotion on this day, so it's kind of hard to talk, frankly," Musk said in a post-launch press conference at NASA's Kennedy Space Center in Florida Saturday evening. "It's been 18 years working towards this goal, so it's hard to believe that it's happened."

Musk's comments came a few hours after SpaceX's Falcon 9 rocket lifted off(opens in new tab) from the center's historic Launch Complex 39A, carrying a Crew Dragon spacecraft with NASA astronauts Bob Behnken(opens in new tab) and Doug Hurley(opens in new tab) on board.By successfully launching its new Crew Dragon spacecraft with astronauts on board for the first time, SpaceX(opens in new tab) became the first private company to launch astronauts for NASA. The test flight, called Demo-2(opens in new tab), is also the first crewed launch from the United States since the space shuttle program ended in 2011. SpaceX and Boeing(opens in new tab) were both selected for NASA's commercial crew program to wean the agency off its dependence on Russia's Soyuz to fly astronauts after the shuttle program was retired.

"I think this is something that's particularly important in the United States but appeals to everyone throughout the world who has within them the spirit of exploration," Musk said. "This is something that I think humanity should be excited about proud of occurring on this day."

If all goes well with the Demo-2 test flight, SpaceX will soon begin launching astronauts to the International Space Station(opens in new tab) (ISS) for NASA as well as other space agencies and private companies. The first operational Crew Dragon mission, called Crew-1(opens in new tab), could launch to the ISS as early as Aug. 30, with three NASA astronauts and one astronaut from the Japanese Aerospace Exploration Agency on board.

This isn't the first time SpaceX has launched a Crew Dragon spacecraft to the ISS. Another Crew Dragon launched to the station in March 2019 for a weeklong demonstration mission called Demo-1, and there were no astronauts on board — only a test dummy named Ripley. Musk was an emotional wreck(opens in new tab) after that mission, too.

Behnken and Hurley will arrive at the ISS Sunday morning (May 30), and the Crew Dragon spacecraft is scheduled to autonomously dock with the orbiting lab at 10:29 a.m. EDT (1429 GMT). You can watch the docking live here on Space.com(opens in new tab), courtesy of NASA TV.

The Demo-2 astronauts, who will be joining the three-person crew of ISS Expedition 63, will spend anywhere from one to four months(opens in new tab) at the station. SpaceX and NASA will determine the duration of their stay after they assess the condition of the Crew Dragon spacecraft in orbit as well as the Crew Dragon that will fly the Crew-1 mission this summer.

When asked about his conversations with the Demo-2 astronauts' kids, Musk — who recently became a dad again(opens in new tab)(he has six sons) — got choked up. "It really hit home," he said of the time he told their two boys that he would do everything in his power to bring their dads home safely.

"I think it was an argument that the return is more dangerous in some ways than the ascent, so in order to declare victory yet, we need to bring them home safely [and] make sure that we're doing everything we can to minimize that risk of reentry and return," Musk said.

You can watch the Demo-2 mission live here and on Space.com's homepage through docking tomorrow (May 31).

## *Elon Musk says he'll have 1,200 ventilators ready to deliver this week*

### *By Mike Wall*

Well, that was fast.

Last Wednesday (March 18), SpaceX and Tesla chief Elon Musk offered to start manufacturing ventilators for coronavirus patients if need be. Medical practitioners and politicians urged him to do so, stressing that many hospitals around the country will have a shortage of breathing machines as the pandemic progresses.

So, Musk's engineers got to work — and they've apparently been very busy.

"We expect to have over ~1,200 [ventilators] to distribute this week. Getting them delivered, installed & operating is the harder part," Musk said via Twitter on Sunday (March 22).

SpaceX and Tesla are both well suited to make ventilators, Musk said last week. After all, every Tesla car features a heating, ventilation and air conditioning system, and SpaceX engineers developed a life-support system for the company's Crew Dragon astronaut taxi, which is scheduled to launch its first crewed mission in May.

That being said, Musk and his teams are still seeking advice from experts.

"Just had a long engineering discussion with Medtronic about state-of-the-art ventilators. Very impressive team!" Musk said in a tweet on Saturday (March 21). (Medtronic builds and sells a variety of medical devices.)

Both SpaceX and Tesla are working on the new ventilators, Musk said. And other companies are doing so as well. On Sunday, for example, President Donald Trump gave Ford and General Motors, along with Tesla, an official manufacturing green light.

Musk is helping hospitals deal with the outbreak in other ways as well. Over the weekend, he told CleanTechnica that his companies will soon start distributing 250,000 N95 masks, critically needed medical respirators that help keep doctors and nurses safe during the outbreak.

Some of this protective gear has already hit the road, making its way to UCLA Health Hospital in Los Angeles and the Seattle home of a doctor at the University of Washington Medical Center who's researching the novel coronavirus and the disease it causes, which is known as COVID-19.

Musk is also offering advice about the outbreak via Twitter. For instance, he has stressed repeatedly that panic about COVID-19 could end up being worse than the disease itself.

## *After 1-Year Joyride in Space, Starman Has Probably Trashed Elon's Roadster*

*By Brandon Specktor*

Starman and his cherry-red Tesla roadster zoom away from Earth in this final photo from the car after its launch on Feb. 6, 2018. A year later, Starman has put more than 470 million miles (760 kilometers) on the odometer and now has Mars in his rearview mirror. (Image credit: SpaceX)

One year ago today (Feb. 6), a spacesuit-clad mannequin named Starman blasted into orbit aboard a cherry-red Tesla roadster he borrowed from his buddy, Tesla and SpaceX founder Elon Musk.

The mannequin and his ride were the first payload aboard the maiden voyage of SpaceX's gargantuan Falcon Heavy rocket. In the past 12 months, car and driver have traveled more than 470 million miles (760 million kilometers) around the sun. They are currently drifting beyond Mars in an elliptical orbit that will last about 557 Earth days, according to the tracking site whereisroadster.com. [7 Everyday Things That Happen Strangely in Space]

Needless to say, the warranty on Starman's Tesla has long since expired ... about 10,000 times over.

According to whereisroadster.com, Starman's roadster has exceed its 36,000-mile (58,000 km) warranty about 13,000 times in the past year. Those numbers might be a little outdated, though; according to Tesla's website, the current warranty for a used roadster is four years or 50,000 miles (80,000 km). So, assuming Starman was able to snag that sweet 2019 rate, he'd have exceeded his warranty about 9,500 times in his travels around the sun so far.

Starman could definitely use that policy, too. As he travels the cosmos in his exposed red convertible, Starman faces an endless barrage of micrometeorites, solar radiation and cosmic rays that will gradually rip his ride (and his spacesuit) to bits. While tiny space rocks dent and ding the car from all sides, the harsh energy of stellar radiation will slash through the carbon-carbon bonds that make up most of the car's plastic, leather and fabric components, chemist William Carroll told Live Science last year.

Organic materials making up the car's leather seats, rubber tires and paints may already be gone. "Those organics, in that environment, I wouldn't give them a year," Carroll said.

A million years from now, the car may be reduced to its naked aluminum frame, but chances are it will still be orbiting the sun. SpaceX initially predicted that Starman and his roadster could cruise the solar system for about 1 billion years.

A study published in 2018 to the preprint journal arXiv.org predicted a slightly shorter life span for the mannequin cosmonaut. According to the study's authors, the car will probably crash into Earth or Venus sometime within the next few tens of millions of years. However, there's just a 6 percent chance that the car will collide with Earth in the next 1 million years and only a 2.5 percent chance it will hit Venus in that same time span.

For now, Starman and his roadster are about 163 million miles (262 million km) beyond Mars and gaining a few thousand miles an hour. It's a long way to go in a year, and the journey has barely begun. We hope Starman has insurance.

## *No More 'BFR': Elon Musk Changes Name of Mars Rocket*

By Mike Wall

Elon Musk is rebranding SpaceX's Mars-colonizing spaceflight system yet again.

The huge, reusable rocket-spaceship duo that SpaceX is building to ferry people to the Red Planet and other celestial destinations will no longer be called the BFR ("Big Falcon Rocket") and BFS ("Big Falcon Spaceship"), respectively.

"Renaming BFR to Starship," Musk announced via Twitter last night (Nov. 19). [The BFR in Images: SpaceX's Giant Spaceship for Mars & Beyond] "Technically, two parts: Starship is the spaceship/upper stage & Super Heavy is the rocket booster needed to escape Earth's deep gravity well (not needed for other planets or moons)," the billionaire entrepreneur added in another tweet.

Musk has had a hard time settling on a name for his Mars spaceflight architecture. He called the initial concept the Mars Colonial Transporter, then changed the moniker to Interplanetary Transport System (ITS) in

2016. ITS became the BFR-BFS in September 2017, when Musk revealed an updated design for the combo.

If "Starship" strikes you as an ambitious moniker, you're not alone; one Twitter user noted that the vehicle will have to journey to another star system to truly earn the name. To which Musk responded: "Later versions will."

More than just the name of the Super Heavy-Starship system is in flux. In September of this year, Musk unveiled a significant new design for the architecture, which makes the spaceship look a lot like the vehicle used by the cartoon character Tintin. Then, just a few days ago, he announced that SpaceX is working on a new design iteration, which he described as a "radical change" and "delightfully counterintuitive," without providing details.

SpaceX's Mars rocket will be the most powerful launcher ever built, and the spaceship will be capable of carrying about 100 people per trip. Together, the vehicles will help get people to the moon, Mars, the Jupiter moon Europa, the Saturn satellite Enceladus and everywhere else they want to go in the solar system, according to Musk's plan.

If everything goes well, the first crewed Mars flight with the system could come in the mid-2020s, Musk has said.

SpaceX also plans to shift all of its business over to the Super Heavy-Starship system eventually. Together, the two vehicles can do everything the company will need to do for the foreseeable future, from launching satellites to cleaning up space junk to carrying passengers on superfast trips from city to city here on Earth.

## *SEC Sues Elon Musk for Fraud Over Twitter Statements About Tesla*

*By Mike Wall*

SpaceX founder and CEO Elon Musk discusses the company's successful Falcon Heavy rocket test launch on Feb. 6, 2018. On Sept. 27, the U.S. Securities and Exchange Commission filed fraud charges against Musk, based on statements he made about perhaps taking his electric-car company, Tesla, private. (Image credit: NASA/Kim Shiflett)

The U.S. Securities and Exchange Commission (SEC) is suing Elon Musk for fraud.

The charges stem from statements Musk made on Aug. 7 indicating that he was considering taking his publicly traded electric-car company, Tesla, private, according to the lawsuit, which was filed today (Sept. 27) in New York.

"Musk's statements, disseminated via Twitter, falsely indicated that, should he so choose, it was virtually certain that he could take Tesla private at a purchase price that reflected a substantial premium over Tesla stock's then-current share price, that funding for this multibillion-dollar transaction had been secured and that the only contingency was a shareholder vote," SEC officials stated in the lawsuit, which you can read.

"In truth and in fact, Musk had not even discussed, much less confirmed, key deal terms, including price, with any potential funding source," SEC officials added. "Musk's false and misleading public statements and omissions caused significant confusion and disruption in the market for Tesla's stock and resulting harm to investors."

The lawsuit does not involve SpaceX, the spaceflight company that Musk founded in 2002 (and for which he serves today as CEO and chief rocket designer).

"This unjustified action by the SEC leaves me deeply saddened and disappointed," Musk said in a statement to CNBC. "I have always taken action in the best interests of truth, transparency and investors. Integrity is the most important value in my life, and the facts will show I never compromised this in any way."

The lawsuit does not involve SpaceX, the spaceflight company that Musk founded in 2002 (and for which he serves today as CEO and chief rocket designer).

"This unjustified action by the SEC leaves me deeply saddened and disappointed," Musk said in a statement to CNBC. "I have always taken action in the best interests of truth, transparency and investors. Integrity is the most important value in my life, and the facts will show I never compromised this in any way."

## *A Japanese Company Says It Will Use SpaceX Rockets to Land on the Moon*

*By Rafi Letzter*

A promotional image from iSpace includes artwork depicting both a rover and a lander. (Image credit: iSpace)

A Japanese company called iSpace announced Wednesday (Sept. 26) that it will launch a lunar lander and lunar rovers to the moon in 2020 and 2021.

The uncrewed iSpace craft will travel to space aboard SpaceX Falcon 9 rockets, the company said. If all goes well, then in 2020, the company will attempt to oribit the moon with one of its landers. In 2021, it will attempt to safely put a lander on the lunar surface and deploy robotic rovers to explore. It's not entirely clear what the landers would search for, but iSpace has indicated in the past that it hopes to find resources, chiefly water, to exploit for future human habitation.

"We share the vision with SpaceX of enabling humans to live in space, so we're very glad they will join us in this first step of our journey," iSpace founder and CEO Takeshi Hakamada said in a statement.SpaceX's own lunar plans involve flying people into the vicinity of the moon in 2023, but it will make no attempt to overcome the technical challenges necessary to conduct a landing.It's worth noting that the last time this company had a deadline for landing on the moon, it didn't meet it. This iSpace two-part mission will take the name HAKUTO-R. "Hakuto" means "white rabbit" in Japanese and refers to Japanese folklore about a rabbit on the moon, the company said. It first used the name as a competitor for Google's never-paid $30 million "Lunar X Prize," which would have been awarded to a company that landed a device on the moon by March 31, 2018. Hakuto, like every other group in the competition, failed to develop a workable device by that date.

## *Japanese Billionaire Will Be First Lunar Tourist. And He Plans to Invite Artists.*

*By Stephanie Pappas*

The Big Falcon Rocket would have three fins and a retractable forward wing, according to an illustration of the rocket's design released by SpaceX's Elon Musk. (Image credit: SpaceX)

Yusaku Maezawa, founder of clothing company ZoZo, will be the first space tourist to travel around the moon, private spaceflight company SpaceX announced tonight (Sept. 17).

"Finally, I can tell you that, 'I choose to go to the moon,'" Maezawa said to cheers in the audience during the press briefing.

Maezawa added, "Ever since I was a kid, I have loved the moon; just staring at the moon filled my imagination; it is always there and has continued to inspire humanity. This is why I cannot pass up this opportunity." And he doesn't want to go alone either. Maezawa said he plans to "go to the moon with artists." He will bring six to eight artists with him, he said.If the trip goes as planned (and SpaceX has stepped back promises of tourist trips to the moon before), Maezawa will zoom toward the moon in 2023 in the newly designed Big Falcon Rocket.

The trip would put the Japanese billionaire and entrepreneur in rarified company, as only 24 people have ever visited the moon, according to NASA. The last time humans made the journey was in 1972, during the Apollo 17 mission crewed by NASA astronauts Eugene Cernan, Harrison Schmitt and Ronald Evans. [The BFR in Images: SpaceX's Giant Spaceship for Mars & Beyond]

The announcement of this trip, is one of many steps SpaceX has taken to realize the company and the Big Falcon Rocket's mission: "To help advance rocket technology to a point where we could potentially become a multi-planet species and a true spacefaring civilization," Elon Musk said during a press briefing tonight.

## *Moon ambitions*

SpaceX CEO Musk first announced that the company would be sending tourists to the moon in February 2017, projecting a 2018 launch date. That mission, which would have used the company's Falcon Heavy rocket and Dragon capsule, never happened. The tourists slated to take that trip were never publically named.

Maezawa founded Japan's largest online shopping mall, Zozotown, according to Forbes. He is also an art collector, shelling out $80 million in 2016 for paintings by Jean-Michel Basquiat and Pablo Picasso, Forbes reported. Forbes named the 42-year-old as No. 18 on its Japan's 50 Richest 2018.

The trip will be expensive. SpaceX did not reveal how much Maezawa paid, but just getting to low-Earth orbit costs a pretty penny. In June, MNN reported, private company Axiom Space announced that starting in 2020, it would be offering 10-day trips to the International Space Station, or ISS, for $55 million a pop.)

Currently, there is no good way for the average Joe or Jane to get to space. According to the travel agency SpaceAdventures, seven space tourists have booked tickets aboard the Russian Soyuz spacecraft to the ISS, but the last of those trips occurred in 2009. Russia halted its space-tourism program in 2010, after the U.S. retired its space shuttle program, leaving fewer seats available to get working astronauts into orbit.

Musk and other private spaceflight CEOs have been striving to fill that gap with spacecraft that can get crews to the ISS and beyond. SpaceX's Falcon 9 rocket and Dragon spacecraft already shuttle cargo back and forth between Earth and the ISS; the company hopes to use its rockets to get humans into space, too. SpaceX announced last month that its first crewed Dragon mission aims to take two NASA astronauts to the ISS in April 2019.

Currently, there is no good way for the average Joe or Jane to get to space. According to the travel agency SpaceAdventures, seven space tourists have booked tickets aboard the Russian Soyuz spacecraft to the ISS, but the last of those trips occurred in 2009. Russia halted its space-tourism program in 2010, after the U.S. retired its space shuttle program, leaving fewer seats available to get working astronauts into orbit.

Musk and other private spaceflight CEOs have been striving to fill that gap with spacecraft that can get crews to the ISS and beyond. SpaceX's Falcon 9 rocket and Dragon spacecraft already shuttle cargo back and forth between Earth and the ISS; the company hopes to use its rockets to get humans into space, too. SpaceX announced last month that its first crewed Dragon mission aims to take two NASA astronauts to the ISS in April 2019.

Currently, there is no good way for the average Joe or Jane to get to space. According to the travel agency SpaceAdventures, seven space tourists have booked tickets aboard the Russian Soyuz spacecraft to the ISS, but the last of those trips occurred in 2009. Russia halted its space-tourism program in 2010, after the U.S. retired its space shuttle program, leaving fewer seats available to get working astronauts into orbit.

Musk and other private spaceflight CEOs have been striving to fill that gap with spacecraft that can get crews to the ISS and beyond. SpaceX's Falcon 9 rocket and Dragon spacecraft already shuttle cargo back and forth between Earth and the ISS; the company hopes to use its rockets to get humans into space, too. SpaceX announced last month that its first crewed Dragon mission aims to take two NASA astronauts to the ISS in April 2019.

## *The BFR*

The ISS orbits 254 miles (408 km) above Earth. The moon's orbit is, on average, 238,855 miles (384,400 km) away. Maezawa will take about three days to reach the moon before orbiting its far side and slingshotting back toward Earth.

To make the trip happen, SpaceX is designing a huge, three-finned Big Falcon Rocket, sometimes known as the "Big F****** Rocket." New renderings released by SpaceX this month show a seven-engine rocket with a separate booster 30 feet (9 meters) in width. It's meant to hold up to 100 passengers on trips as far away as Mars.

And if you were wondering, "We'll do a bunch of test launches before having any people on board," Musk said.

## *Tesla on Autopilot Crashes into Parked Police Car*

*By Yasemin Saplakoglu*

On Tuesday, a Tesla sedan on autopilot crashed into a parked police cruiser in Laguna Beach, California (Image credit: Uncredited/AP/Rex/Shutterstock)

The idea that self-driving cars will be much safer than human drivers has been taking a hit lately with a string of autopilot crashes, the latest incident in California this week.

A Tesla Sedan crashed into an empty, parked police car in Laguna Beach on Tuesday (May 29) while running on semi-autonomous autopilot. The driver who was behind the wheel experienced minor injuries, according to the Associated Press.

Sergeant Jim Cota of the Laguna Beach Police Department said the car was totaled, so he was thankful no one was in it, according to the Los Angeles Times. Cota added that a year ago, in the same area, there was a similar instance of a Tesla crashing into a semi-truck. This follows a trail of other autopilot crashes including one in Utah of a driver looking at her phone while riding in a Tesla on autopilot, a fatal accident in California of a Tesla Model X crashing into a barrier in March, and another fatal Tesla crash in Florida in 2016 — the first known Tesla autopilot crash, according to the Los Angeles Times .

According to the Times, Tesla has warned drivers that they need to stay alert and keep their hands on the wheel when on autopilot mode. They also make drivers accept a dialogue box that says this mode is only designed for use on highways with a "center divider and clear lane markings," a Tesla spokesperson told the Times.

But it's not only Tesla's autopilot that has been causing trouble lately. Last March, an Uber self-driving car killed a pedestrian in Arizona as she was crossing the street. According to a preliminary report released by the National Transportation Safety Board last week, the Uber system detected the woman 6 seconds before hitting her, first identifying her as an unknown object, then as a vehicle, and finally as a bicycle (she was walking a bike across the street). Then, 1.3 seconds before the crash, the autopilot system recognized that an emergency brake would be necessary to avoid a crash; the way the autonomous Uber system was set up, it didn't allow for such emergency braking maneuvers and expected the driver to take control, yet didn't issue any warnings.The seeming spate of accidents may make self-driving cars seem like menaces. Granted, the sample size for autonomous vehicle accidents is much smaller than human-caused vehicles crashes — those are so common that most are not reported in the news. In 2016, 37,461 people died because of traffic-related accidents in the United States, according to the New York Times. Most researchers tend to think self-driving cars will still be safer, but that they are in their experimental stages, according to the NY Times.

## *SpaceX's Elon Musk Proposes Media Company That Rates Journalists. Is He Serious?*

*By Elizabeth Howell*

Elon Musk speaks at the Tesla Design Studio on April 30, 2015, in Hawthorne, California. (Image credit: Kevork Djansezian/Getty Images)

SpaceX founder Elon Musk just said on Twitter that he wants to start a new media outlet. What's behind his posts? Is it just another Musk prank, or is he actually serious about the idea?

"The holier-than-thou hypocrisy of big media companies who lay claim to the truth, but publish only enough to sugarcoat the lie, is why the public no longer respects them," Musk posted Wednesday (May 23) along with a link to a news story discussing negative media coverage of his electric car company, Tesla.

Musk then wrote a series of tweets lamenting the state of journalism and vowing to do something about it.

"Problem is," he said, "journos are under constant pressure to get max clicks & earn advertising dollars or get fired. Tricky situation, as Tesla doesn't advertise, but fossil fuel companies & gas/diesel car companies are among world's biggest advertisers."

Musk said he plans to start up a new website for the public to rate "the core truth of any article" that would also track credibility scores for journalists, editors and publications. He said he may call it "Pravda," which was the name of the former Soviet Union Communist Party newspaper. "Pravda" means "truth" in Russian.

"Even if some of the public doesn't care about the credibility score, the journalists, editors & publications will. It is how they define themselves," Musk said. He then created a Twitter poll asking readers if they would be in support of that or not. By the time the poll closed today (May 24), it had received more than 680,000 votes, with 88 percent of voters saying they would support Musk's proposal.

Musk urged the media to promote the poll if "they didn't want Pravda to exist," then tweeted again, saying he may call the site "You're Right" instead. Musk does own the domain youreright.com, he added, but all it does now is point to Facebook News.

"For some reason, this is the best I've felt in a while. Hope you're feeling good too," Musk added.

But as The Wall Street Journal pointed out, Musk is famous for making proclamations that may not necessarily be serious. For example, in recent posts, he claimed that Tesla was going bankrupt (that was posted on April Fools' Day); that he was going to start a candy company; and that he was going to start a new company to drill tunnels to avoid traffic. (That last one may not have been a joke; Musk eventually started a new tunneling organization called The Boring Co., whose goal is to build an underground Hyperloop transportation system.)

Musk's comments, naturally, attracted attention on Twitter from everybody from journalists to Donald Trump Jr., the son of U.S. President Donald Trump.

"One journalist retweeted Mr. Musk's comments with a link to a California filing for a business incorporated last October called Pravda Corp.," The Wall Street Journal added, "involving a person connected with other Musk ventures. 'Er, he's not kidding,' wrote journalist Mark Harris. Mr. Musk replied with a "hugging face" emoji.

## *Does Humanity Need a Backup Earth?*

*By Elizabeth Howell*

SpaceX CEO Elon Musk has a vision: He wants to get humans to Mars as soon as possible. He already wowed the world this year, when the Falcon Heavy launched and flung a Tesla car toward the asteroid belt. And this heavy-lift rocket will be dwarfed by the boosters Musk plans for Mars exploration, which he says will carry colonists in fleets of ships to the Red Planet.

While getting to Mars is an end in itself, there's another compelling reason to go. Science fiction is full of dystopian futures for Earth if humanity remains limited to this planet. There are the asteroid strikes of the "Deep Impact" and "Armageddon" films, the robot wars of the "Battlestar Galactica" TV series and "Terminator" film franchise, the medical problems and overpopulation in the "Children of Men" and "Elysium" movies, and many other disasters natural and artificial. Dark futures and colonizing other planets is covered in "AMC Visionaries: James Cameron's Story of Science Fiction," which ran its fourth episode May 21.Science fiction inspired the first rocket pioneers to explore beyond Earth. Robert Goddard, who pushed forward liquid rocketry in the early 1900s, was clearly a fan of the genre, because he wrote some science fiction himself, according to io9. The Apollo moon rockets of the 1960s and 1970s were designed by Wernher von Braun, who enjoyed science fiction as a child and partnered with Disney in the 1950s to create educational films about spaceflight. [Gallery: Visions of Interstellar Starship Travel]

And a quick glance around the solar system shows us one real-life reason scientists — and indeed, all of us — should take a page from science fiction and be concerned about Earth's future. The moon, Mars and many of the "airless" moons around the neighborhood are littered with craters. These came from space rocks and other small worlds that slammed into the moon's and planet's surfaces over billions of years.

Lest you imagine that Earth is immune because of its thick atmosphere, think of the dinosaurs, felled about 66 million years ago when a large asteroid or comet around 10 to 15 kilometers (6.2 to 9.3 miles) in diameter slammed into the Earth. We also just passed the five-year anniversary of Chelyabinsk, when a 17-meter (56 feet) small body exploded over a town in Russia, causing many injuries and property damage from shattered glass.

NASA does have an active asteroid-search program and some plans for dealing with asteroids menacing Earth, but even preparing for those intruders isn't enough; there's another, bigger inevitable threat to our planet. In about 4 billion years or 5 billion years, the sun will swell into a red giant after it consumes all of its hydrogen and begins fusing helium. As the star expands, it will swallow up Mercury and Venus and get close to Earth. Our planet will be roasted to a crisp, thrown out of its orbit or swallowed altogether. In any of these scenarios, that's bad news for humans and life on Earth in general.

## *Get your a— to Mars*

One popular destination for escaping Earth in science fiction is Mars. At first, this was because people thought other beings like us may live there. In 1877, Italian astronomer Giovanni Schiaparelli reported observing channels on Mars, but stopped short of saying whether they were natural or artificial. U.S. science popularizer Percival Lowell, however, went much further in the early 1900s, coming up with explanations as to why the channels were there. Perhaps the Martians were trying to drain water to support a dying planet, Lowell said. (The channels, or canals, were later explained as telescope artifacts when robotic missions to Mars showed the formations don't exist.)

This turn-of-the-century musing greatly influenced science fiction of the era. There was the famous "War of the Worlds" novel by H.G. Wells in 1898, which portrayed a Martian invasion of Earth. (It was recapped in a 1938 national radio broadcast, as well as a 2005 film starring Tom Cruise.) Also, Edgar Rice Burroughs published "A Princess of Mars" in 1912, kicking off a series about Mars (which he called Barsoom) full of living beings.

(The widely panned 2012 movie "John Carter" was based on some of these stories.) [Film Review: 'War of the Worlds' Update Hits Home]

Robert Zubrin, founder of the human exploration advocacy group The Mars Society, told Space.com that Mars will someday be an inhabited planet as science fiction writers envisioned. As only two examples of many showing that future, there's the 2015 Matt Damon movie "The Martian" or the 1990 Arnold Schwarzenegger film "Total Recall," which included the famous line, "Get your a— to Mars."

But why does science fiction make exploration look so much easier than we find in real life? Zubrin said, in part, it's because of our mindset.

"Here we are, 500 years or so after [Nicolaus] Copernicus [who said Earth orbits the sun], and most people still talk about the Earth as the world, and there's a thing above us called the sky. Most people still have this geocentric viewpoint," Zubrin told Space.com, pointing out that Earth is in space and we rarely think about that fact in our everyday lives.

Zubrin said our approach of going to Mars via low Earth orbit and the moon is incremental. This approach to space exploration, he said, is similar to telling Lewis and Clark to just go 100 miles (160 kilometers) out beyond the Mississippi River and to wait for the next group of explorers to move farther west.

"If someone asks you why space is so important, it's comparative to somebody in a small village somewhere saying, 'Why is the rest of the world important?' which is sort of an absurd question," Zubrin said. So, he advocates going elsewhere in search of resources, knowledge or a safe haven that we couldn't find on Earth. Interstellar travel would be the ultimate dream, Zubrin said, but in the meantime, we should focus on what we have at hand: Mars, which is close enough to visit using today's technology.

"The most important step is deciding that you want to do it. This is really the dramatic step that Elon Musk is taking," Zubrin said. "There are people at NASA who want to do it, but as an institution, it has been dragging its feet and providing every excuse to the political class not to embrace the challenge."

## *Moving to Mars — or beyond?*

Zubrin's plan (which he outlined in a 1991 paper called "Mars Direct," and which he has expanded on greatly since then) advocates for a direct flight to Mars, with minimal or no on-orbit assembly of the spacecraft. Using current propulsion systems, a spacecraft could get to the Red Planet in six months — the standard rotation astronauts spend on the International Space Station, Zubrin pointed out.

The first missions would bring most of the supplies those travelers would need to live, such as food and water. But the early trips could also bring along architecture so later missions could do more "living off the land," such as greenhouses or habitats. (The first Mars voyagers may eat more meat brought with them, while future generations would be more vegetarian due to the resources on hand, Zubrin said.) He said the habitats of the Mars Society's Mars Desert Research Station and Flashline Mars Arctic Research Station are designed to preview what real Red Planet homes could look like.

The return vehicle would include propellant made from Martian carbon dioxide and water, specifically to generate the fuels methane and oxygen. Zubrin said it's the cheapest propellant combination, with only a hydrogen-oxygen mix providing better exhaust velocity.

But there's a big problem with Mars — it's not very much like Earth. Sure, people could conceivable live on it with technology to manage the risks. Its day is similar in length to Earth's day, too. But the planet has only one-third of Earth's gravity. Martian air isn't breathable. Water, if it exists at all on the surface, would be in scarce quantities. Conditions are even worse on the moon, which has one-sixth Earth's gravity, a longer day-night cycle than our home planet and no air whatsoever.

"They're not places that we are necessarily going to colonize in large numbers," Roger Launius, a retired curator from the Smithsonian Institution's National Air and Space Museum, told Space.com. He predicted that by the end of the century, there may be research stations at the moon or Mars, similar to what exists now in Antarctica.

But to really find another home for humanity, we'll have to follow the lead of "Battlestar Galactica" and search for another Earth. Because, otherwise, children are going to be born in lunar or Martian environments that have a lesser gravity than Earth. How this will affect their development when humans are built for Earth is an unknown, Launius said.But quickly getting to other stars, where second Earths may exist, will be slow unless we figure out a method for faster-than-light speed, or a way to sustain a spacecraft over multiple generations, Launius said. Another possibility is to extend astronaut life spans through hibernation (as done in the movies "Alien" and "Avatar") or by becoming a sort of "Star Trek"-like Borg that would integrate robotics into the human body to extend lives.

## *This Horrifying AI Thought Experiment Got Elon Musk a Date*

*By Stephanie Pappas*

Enter Caption

Elon Musk and musician Grimes show up as a couple to the 2018 Met Gala on May 7 at the Metropolitan Museum of Art in New York. (Image credit: ANGELA WEISS/AFP/Getty Images)

It's Elon Musk at his Elon Musk-iest: According to news reports, the space-and-electric-car entrepreneur met his current girlfriend by making a joke about treacherous artificial intelligence.

Musk and the musician Grimes, whose real name is Claire Boucher, went to the Met Gala as a couple Monday (May 7). According to the gossip publication Page Six, the two met via Twitter, when Musk thought to make a pun about "Rococo's Basilisk," a mashup of the thought experiment "Roko's Basilisk" and the elaborately ornamental style seen in 18th-century France.

Musk soon learned that Grimes had made the same pun in a music video in 2015, and the rest is romantic history. Roko's Basilisk, on the other hand, is a terrifying vision of the future and the center of a yearslong online subculture maelstrom.The whole thing got started in 2010, when a person going by Roko posted a thought experiment to the site LessWrong, a forum where people discuss everything from philosophy to artificial intelligence (AI) to cognitive science. The post was deleted, but RationalWiki preserved a copy. Roko's idea was that if, in the future, a super-intelligent AI designed to maximize the common good were to come into being, it might punish everyone who didn't contribute to its existence.

"Of course, this would be unjust, but it is the kind of unjust thing that is oh-so-very utilitarian," Roko reasoned.

This hypothetical would take place after the singularity, the point at which artificial intelligence becomes indistinguishable from life itself — in fact, better than life itself, because it can do things like upload itself indefinitely, achieving a kind of silicon immortality. If this godlike power discovers you didn't help create it, well, sheesh. It might just decide that your just reward is eternal torment. [A Brief History of Artificial Intelligence]

The "basilisk" name came from a medieval legend about a snake that could kill with a glance.

Here's the trap, though: If you didn't know about the possibility of Roko's Basilisk, you're in the clear — the AI is only likely to come after those who predicted its existence but chose not to, say, donate all their disposable income to help bring it about. Just by reading about the possibility of Roko's Basilisk, you've doomed yourself.

"Of course, this would be unjust, but it is the kind of unjust thing that is oh-so-very utilitarian," Roko reasoned.

This hypothetical would take place after the singularity, the point at which artificial intelligence becomes indistinguishable from life itself — in fact, better than life itself, because it can do things like upload itself indefinitely, achieving a kind of silicon immortality. If this godlike power discovers you didn't help create it, well, sheesh. It might just decide that your just reward is eternal torment. [A Brief History of Artificial Intelligence]

The "basilisk" name came from a medieval legend about a snake that could kill with a glance.

Here's the trap, though: If you didn't know about the possibility of Roko's Basilisk, you're in the clear — the AI is only likely to come after those who predicted its existence but chose not to, say, donate all their disposable income to help bring it about. Just by reading about the possibility of Roko's Basilisk, you've doomed yourself.

## *From Roko to romance*

The ban on Roko's Basilisk discussion on LessWrong lasted until 2015. Yudkowsky later wrote on Reddit that he regretted his reaction, which made it seem like he thought Roko was right; he actually believes that no artificial intelligence designed with humanity's best interests in mind would end up torturing people. Instead, he wrote, he deleted the post because the idea had no potential benefit to anyone.

Musk might be particularly fond of Roko's Basilisk's jokes because the original post mentioned him. Roko writes that someone like Musk, who is "single-handedly changing the faces of high-impact industries," would be in the good graces of the theoretical superhuman AI. Musk has also been vocal about the potential dangers of AI, calling for regulation and warning just last month that AI could become an "immortal dictator."

"If AI has a goal and humanity just happens to be in the way, it will destroy humanity as a matter of course without even thinking about it. No hard feelings," Musk said in a documentary called "Do You Trust This Computer?," which was released in April. "It's just like, if we're building a road, and an anthill happens to be in the way. We don't hate ants, we're just building a road. So, goodbye, anthill."Grimes, for her part, is a Canadian musician and visual artist who came up with the "Rococo Basilisk" pun for her music video "Flesh Without Blood." The video features a character who wears Rococo-style wigs and voluminous dresses and ends up stabbed in the gut and covered in blood on a tennis court.

9 798887 490038

Printed by Libri Plureos GmbH in Hamburg,
Germany